Dining at Downton

Traditions of the Table From The Unofficial Guide to Downton Abbey

Elizabeth Fellow

Table of Contents

Introduction – You're Invited to the Abbey

Deeply engrossed in a book, you are curled up by the fire. The door to the drawing room opens, and in walks James, your family butler. Silver tray in hand, he walks over to the sofa.

"An invitation from The Abbey M'Lady"

Genteelly, he bends at the waist, allowing you to take the beautifully handwritten card to read.

An invitation to dine with the Crawley's. How incredibly exciting! The date on the card is 13th July 1924. Naturally they will dine at 8pm. Of course, you must go. There is nothing to decide. You are eager to see for yourself if all the stories you have heard about its opulence and grandeur are true.

Closing your book, you seat yourself at your bureau to prepare your reply. If you hurry, James can catch the post before four.

But even with pen it in hand and paper on the blotter, you feel the fizzing bubble of excitement to be invited to the house. Famous not only for its sumptuous food but also the family's ability to be in exactly the right place at the right time (and wearing exactly the right thing!), Downton Abbey is the place everyone wants to be seen.

It seems, my darling, you have made it!

Closing your eyes, the excitement is almost too much to contain. But then uncertainty rears its head….

What should you wear? Should you get your hair done or will your maid's finger wave expertise be glamorous enough?

Goodness, what on earth will everyone be talking about? What if the conversation comes round to something you nothing about? The last thing you want to do is get it wrong!

In your reverie, you remember some of the snippets you have gleaned from others who have made it to the house. Descriptions of ingredients many of us can only dream of. Caviar, oysters, Champagne, rich and lavish banquets abound.

You seldom eat out, and so this invitation is such a treat. Your own cook Mrs Lacey has always provided first-rate food at home, but an invitation to the Abbey feels like it is in a different league. Powerful bachelors, elegant beauties, and sumptuous food all lit through crystal and candlelight.

Relax, my beauty, because *"**Dining at Downton**"* will relate, not just the most beautiful recipes, but where the food has come from, the politics of time, the fashions, fragrances, and flavours of the period.

Come with me to a world more lavish, more beautiful, and more carefully created than we might ever experience today. Together let's prepare for Dining at Downton.

Dining at Downton – the Etiquette, the Food, and Where it Came From

If afternoon tea was the ladies' social gathering, dinner, in the 1920s, was a far more powerful thing. For allegiances were created, societal manoeuvres were performed, and commercial (and romantic) alliances were built in the dining room of Downton Abbey, all performed with blithe smiles and with the most subtle finesse.

Carson and his footmen discretely placed beautifully prepared meals in front of guests, each dish designed to secure the estate with ever more promise of success. Mrs Patmore and Daisy created culinary masterpieces that would ensure guests would continue to visit and deal with the family for many years to come. This was networking on the very grandest of scales.

The intricate arrangement of the menu and the dinner itself was a feat of great co-ordination. Mrs Patmore, creating a suggested menu from the seasonal vegetables in the garden and conversations with the butcher and gamekeeper, would keep a very tight rein on the budget. Her suggested menu would then be taken to her Ladyship who was a font of all knowledge about likes, dislikes, and taste buds of her guests! It would be at her behest that more exotic dishes might come to the table.

A good cook's objective was always be to optimise the amount of yield she could get from any one ingredient. Beef then, would come to the Abbey complete with the organs and bones of the beast as well as the regular cuts of meat. A carcass would always be boiled up to produce ever more wonderful stock. Entrées in particular, would often feature what we would term as offal these days, the innards, the liver, kidneys, and heart. These cheap cuts were turned into exquisitely light dishes, often served with potatoes and a deliciously rich sauce.

The wild Yorkshire countryside is wonderful farming country, and much of the food eaten at the table came from the working estate. Many of Lady Mary's pigs, of course, would eventually become bacon (*bless them*) as well as other fine cuts of meat such as the York Ham in the recipe later. Nothing was ever left over from a good animal. In Christmas at Downton, I list a recipe for brawn, the favourite dish for using up the trotters and pig's head!

In the twenties, fish courses were standard fare in the menu. This was game in plenty, as the rivers in the area team with stock. With fishing ports like Whitby and Scarborough less than 50 miles away, sea fish were easily available too. Herring, cod, haddock, prawn, mussels, crabs, oysters, and lobsters were all considered local foods hailing from East Yorkshire.

In England, seasonality has as much to do with hunting restrictions as it does with what is ready to harvest (mainly to protect the younger animals in the spring). The collaboration between the game keeper and Mrs Patmore ensured that as much of the money going out of the kitchen went back into the coffers of the estate, with a smaller portion going to the butcher. However, legal restrictions dictated what could find its way to the table and when.

In Yorkshire, duck and goose can be hunted between September and January. "The Glorious 12th" marks the celebrated opening of the Grouse season in August and ends on 10th December. Hares can be shot between 1st August and 29th February. Partridges were often served up on plates between the beginning of September and the end of January. Pheasant has a shorter year, available between 1st October and 1st February, making it a wintertime favourite delicacy.

Quail, wood pigeon, and rabbits were shot and served all year round.

The availability of venison is always good in England (although expensive), but shooting is limited to hunting bucks between August and April, and does between November and February. Being such a heavy meat, it was not missed when not available for lighter spring menus.

Estates of the day also provided dairy from the cattle, to be churned into milk, cream, and butter. We do not ever see a dairy maid on screen potentially because she was always out in the dairy, or otherwise huddled by the fire keeping warm! Dairies of the period were punishingly cold, tiled from floor to ceiling. Churning the butter and constantly washing away the whey was cold and exhausting work.

Although some cheese would be made in the dairy, not all of it would come from the house, as it was too labour-intensive to create on a large scale. Visitors to the house, then, would enjoy not only national treasures such as Cheddar and Stilton but also Yorkshire's own local Wensleydale cheese too (of Wallace and Gromit fame!)

In some ways, we have come full circle. As a generation, we feeling the ebbs and flows of the seasons more in our eating again, but it is a different experience. For their generation, there was no choice. You ate what was in season, because that's what there was. There was no big secret to it. In the same way, it was important for the ingredients to work as hard as they could. Products like Espagnole Sauce were larder staples to extend the crops further through the year. The same applies for the apricot jam in Crème de Surprise. In these dishes, nature had been captured in the autumn to put taste and goodness into the dishes over the winter. The entrées and desserts were always created with what we would consider to be leftovers, and what they saw as bounty. The main course, or the "remove" as it was more correctly referred to, was made of a prime cut or the main part of the beast that could be relied upon to feed as many people in one sitting as possible. Left overs were used for the next day's meal or for dinner for downstairs. .

As with any household, there were those with more exotic taste buds than others, both upstairs and down. The staff in the house grew to have extremely refined palates, eating leftovers of some of the most elaborate meals. In her Book "The Downstairs Cookbook," Margaret Powell describes how she had to settle for a different way of eating when she married and left the great house, where she had been a cook.

"When I married the milkman, who earned a wage of £3 5s a week, I had to come down from eating butter to margarine, from rump steak to shin of beef or stewing steak, and from cream to evaporated milk. I was able to accept it easily because we were taught we were not with 'them' or of 'them,' that our worlds were apart in every way. We didn't ally ourselves to the kind of eating and comfort they had. We were made to feel different, and we *felt* different."

(£3 5s 0d – Three pounds five shillings was about equal to £170 in today's money. For my American friends that equals about $265 a week.)

And yet, it was always the downstairs expertise running the show. Choosing the perfect matching wine for each dish was an art in itself, and that fell to Carson and his drinks knowledge. Predominately, the choices hailed from the chalky slopes of Burgundy and Bordeaux in France, as well as Champagne from Reims. Hors d'oeuvres were served with Sherry from Spain and cheeses with Port from Portugal. With the dawn of a more adventurous spirit of cocktail parties, naturally his knowledge also had to grow with G & Ts and vodka introducing their own Charleston kicks.

The mainstay of the ingredients would come from the Estate, as we have seen, but just occasionally, it might be necessary for a little something special to come from further afield. The spices and caviar you see in this book are good examples of these. These had been integrated into the upper class palate over the last 20 years or so as people had travelled (for work or leisure) to far off more exotic climes of the British Empire. Now more easily accessible than they had previously been, there was no longer a need to keep spices under lock and key. However, many kitchens now housed ornate spice chests of many drawers which were only for the cook to touch.

By far the biggest influence on the English kitchen though was the French. Indeed, whilst many of the name of the dishes are in English now, they were referred to by their French terminology. This practice had come from the kitchens of the very first celebrity chef, Marie Antoine Careme, who had worked for some of the finest royalty in Europe, from Napoleon to George IV. At the most elaborate dinners, a menu would be placed in front of each guest detailing the entirety of the meal in French. A family occasion, though, naturally would be a less formal affair. Compare this splendid feast against the simplicity of the short, snappy, and sassy cocktail party. No wonder the youthful aristocracy would rather enjoy the new trendy way to meet.

In Christmas at Downton, we examined the intricate etiquette of how the table was laid, so without further ado, let's choose the correct wine glass. Champagne, my darling, is the furthest one away from you. The one above your soup spoon is white wine. Next to that is red, and your champagne flute is the one above that…got it? Let's raise a toast to the beautiful dishes of the Downton Abbey dinner party.

Elizabeth Fellow

The Social Aspects of Dining – Politics and Business, Fashion, and Changing Times

As series 5 opens (in 1924), it is fascinating to see how both upstairs and downstairs are aware of the societal changes afoot. Dinner, as we see it in this book, will very soon be a thing of the past. By 1935 serving entrées was considered very much passé. Whilst the recipes will remain with us, the splendour, pomp, and circumstance is very quickly slipping through the fingers of everyone at the great house. Interestingly, it is downstairs who seem most reticent of the change.

Probably the biggest threat to the Abbey's status quo was to also be its greatest opportunity. Tom Branson, the caddish chauffeur who had seduced Lady Sybil, has brought socialist ideals into an extremely conservative environment. He, along with Mary Crawley, is set to create a whole new dynamic world for the future that the aristocracy must face. The gentle and indulged life they have known is clearly changing, and because of his influences, the house is ready to move with it.

The rules of conversation at the dinner table with other landowners and dignitaries of the period were changing to. Previously, one absolutely did not speak of politics, religion, or money at the table. Chatter had been light and entertaining. Now, however, life cannot be so straightforward for the family, and new networks must be built.

Where the war had so recently been the only subject on everyone's lips, now, in England, politics had taken its place. What was happening inside the parliamentary walls of Westminster was to threaten not only the wealth of the landowners but the blue collar manual workers as well. No one could be deaf to the rumblings outside of Downton's doors.

This is the year Ramsey McDonald walked through the famous door of Number 10 Downing Street. Great Britain steeled itself for radical change. McDonald, England's first ever Labour Prime Minister, had won the seat from Stanley Baldwin, whose government had been ousted after a vote of no confidence. The perspective of the country was changing. There was a lobbying for rights for the working classes.

Previously, McDonald had been Chairman of his party, but in 1918 he had been defeated because of dissent against his opposition to the war. England, in her fickle way, had a very short memory, and in '24 elected him to the premier's position. His stint in power was to be short lived, however. Just nine months later though, trouble was at his door.

A communist newspaper had published a letter from a young activist named J R Campbell, inciting mutiny in the military ranks. It claimed that most people had not signed up to fight in the war because they wanted to battle but rather as a dissenting vote against the high levels of poverty and unemployment. They suggested that, instead of taking up arms against other countries, they should instead rally against the capitalist oppressors of their own country.

On 6th August, the Attorney General announced that charges should be brought against Campbell, but a week later the government bowed to back bencher pressure, and the charges were dropped. England's common man was furious, and a General Election was called. Labour's moment of glory was well and truly over (that is until McDonald was re-elected in 1929). The year 1926 saw 1.7 million workers come out in the 10-day General Strike in support of coal miners and their working conditions.

The world was getting smaller, and people's rights were changing. Emeline Parkhurst and her brave ladies were fighting for equality for women. In fact, McDonald's government appointed Margaret Bondfield as the first ever female Cabinet Minister when she was made Parliamentary Secretary.

The "ordinary person" was gaining more rights across the board. One of the reasons for this was the advent of greater education. The school-leaving age had recently been introduced. In 1917, it became mandatory for every child to complete schooling to the age of 14. (This was raised to 15 in '47 and 16 in '72.)

These social changes rippled all across the British Empire, right over to the Eastern world. Just as workers were being encouraged to take up arms in London City, so comrades across the world united. In 1917, the Russian Revolution ejected the aristocracy from their homeland, and murdered many members of the Russian royal family. The extended, impoverished royal family were refugees in England. It must have seemed a dark and foreboding place. Nevertheless, Russian dignitaries could often be found at parties, attractive for their romantic and bohemian tales.

Most certainly all dinner conversation in July of this year would be full of the Scottish athlete Eric Liddell. A staunch Christian, Liddell had gone to the Paris Olympics only to find he could not compete in his favoured event of 100 meters because the event fell on a Sunday. Instead he ran in the 400 meters, in which he subsequently won gold, gaining a world record of 47.6 seconds. It was one of nine gold, thirteen silver, and 12 bronze medals for the country.

England stood proud in the Liddells victory, made even sweeter for British born Jew Harold Abrahams still winning gold for his country in the 100m.

The political shift of course, also promises economic changes for the house, and his Lordship is all too aware the rules his mother, the dowager Duchess, and his late father had played by, will no longer cut it if Downton Abbey is to stay in his family's hands. It is a brave stance he takes, inviting newly powerful people to his dinner table in a bid to build relationships with, not only old money, but with the nouveaux riches and foreign dignitaries too.

This acceptance ran bitterly throughout classes of all levels for many years to come. Even as a child, my *own* mother would virtually spit "nouveaux riches" with absolute disdain. To her, it regaled bad manners, ill breeding. It seemed to completely explain away crass behaviour. *Parvenu*: they would be referred to, using the terminology meaning "to arrive". The class divide in England was becoming ever more blurred.

Reader, do you remember poor Julia Roberts in Pretty Woman and her bewilderment over what knife should be used for what? Give a passing thought to these newly arrived people, who had worked very hard to equal his Lordship in money and status, but who would not be naturally well versed in the silent language of the napkin. It was no longer considered correct to tuck it into the neck of one's collar, but rather lay it on ones lap. Where should one put it if called away to the telephone, for example? Aunt Violet would surely roll her eyes in contempt if the napkin found its way to the table when its owner left, because it should be placed on the seat.

Harder still were the muted signals that made it simple for Carson and the footmen to know when to clear the table. If one placed one's knife and fork together at four o'clock position on the plate, it signalled you were finished and the plate could be taken away. The knife, placed at four and the fork at eight, apart on the plate, meant you were intending to carry on and were merely taking a pause in your chewing. A wrongly placed knife and fork could leave people sitting for several awkward minutes before his Lordship would have to signal to Carson, that he was happy for the plates to be cleared.

In fact, it was always his Lordship who would give the silent cues to the staff. No one could be seated until he and Lady Cora had taken their places. It was only then that the footmen would open the chairs for everyone else. Likewise, should either the Earl or Countess have reason to leave the table early, it was correct that everyone else at the table should stand. At the end of the evening, it was a nod from Lady Cora to the rest of the ladies to leave the table and retire to the drawing room for coffee whilst the men took a turn playing cards.

So, whilst there are starched cloths and sparkling silver on the table, there is an undercurrent starting to rumble. Life at the Abbey is ripe for change. Luckily, the family is ready to embrace it and draws these changes into its midst. The pragmatic Lady Mary and forthright Countess are always ready to welcome opportunities to drive the business of Downton forward.

The food, for instance, starts to take on a slightly Bolshevik twist with Beef Stroganoff, caviar, and borscht. Dinner at Downton has always been elegant and cosmopolitan, showcasing ingredients from across the Empire, but these exotic eastern dishes became particular favourites to dine.

The odd Martini becomes shaken (not stirred) as quicker and far sassier cocktail parties are risked in the dining room.

These of course, were particularly relished by American cousins, who were enduring tedious prohibition back home!

When Rose gleefully declares "I love cocktail parties," Cora risks an uncharacteristically barbed remark saying, 'Me too. You only have to stay 40 minutes, instead of sitting through seven courses stuck between a half-deaf landowner and an even deafer major general.'

These parties showcased the most glamorous aspect of the period, the beautiful dresses. We see the very first herald of what would later become known as the cocktail dress. Long gowns are out and knee length flapper frocks are well and truly in. Sumptuously beaded, these androgynous dresses oozed sex appeal. It was said a good flapper would never sit down for fear of spoiling her dress. The joy of the garment was in its movement, designed for ultimate body freedom, with many having wonderful fringing causing avalanches of swing. These magnificent feats of beadwork meant that the sassiest girl would be likely to turn down a dinner invitation in favour of cocktails where she could more comfortably stand.

The very best cocktail parties might have a familiar scent of Chanel Number 5 hanging in the air. Coco Chanel and Ernest Beaux had created a fragrance entirely for the flapper generation. Even the bottle was stripped down to its essence and was completely transparent, unlike the opaque beauties that had gone before.

For the most cosmopolitan of flappers, there was a whisper on the wind of a rather risqué dance being flicked and kicked in South Carolina. The Charleston made its appearance in 1923. In 1926 it would be seen at no lesser place than the Follie Bergers where Josephine Baker would shock the world with her gay abandon. Strangely, the famous dance only really existed in the public consciousness for a year, but in 1926 any flapper worth her salt would have the famous Charleston swivel step down to the finest of arts. And just as quick as it came, it was gone.

Twelve months from now, at the 1925 Expo, what would decades later be called Art Deco exploded onto the scene. There was an explosion of colour and shapes that changed British design as we know it. Already though, since 1920, these new geometric lines have been filtering through. In the late 19th century Art Nouveau had been romantic, fluid, and opulent. Suddenly art and expression was stark and symmetrical...and of course hairstyles immediately followed. The bobbed hair cut made so famous by Louise Brookes in 1925 saw an earlier introduction on the coiffured head of one of the Downton stars described as looking "Half Vogue model, half stick of dynamite!"

The wireless, which has been so richly anticipated at Downton, comes into its own in 1924 with the first ever shipping forecast. Yorkshire had an abundant fishing community, and this was gratefully received. The forecast would go on to save many thousands of the Abbey's neighbours' lives.

In February, the wireless also began to broadcast hourly signals from Greenwich, allowing pocket watches across the country to keep far more accurate times.

Politics and fashion aside, the star of the show in Downton Abbey was definitely the food brought to the dining room from the kitchen. Each dish was carefully carried from the steamy kitchen below, up the stairs, and along the long corridor to the table. The pristine white gloves and starched collars of the butler and footmen completed the elegant procession.

The Recipes of Dining at Downton Entrées

(or Appetizers as our American friends call them)

Potato Blinis with Red Caviar

Ingredients:

- 10 large potatoes
- 4 whole eggs
- 1/3 (80ml) cup milk
- 1/4 tsp salt
- 2 Tbsp flour
- 4 Tbsp canola oil
- 13 Tbsp natural red salmon caviar (about 12 tbs)
- 1 cup (270ml) sour cream
- 1 Tbsp finely chopped chives

Directions:

1. Peel and cut the potatoes into small pieces to allow them to cook evenly and quickly. Place them into a heavy pan, and cover with cold water. Bring to the boil, and then reduce to a simmer. Cover and leave to cook for around 30 minutes or until tender. Drain.
2. Mrs Patmore would have pressed her potatoes through a food mill, but a masher works just as effectively. Mince the potatoes finely.
3. Add two eggs, and whisk together fully.
4. Add slightly warmed milk, and season with salt.
5. Place a baking sheet to heat in the oven.

6. Heat a skillet over a high flame, and add a drizzle of oil.
7. Drizzle about a 1/4 of cup of the blini mixture, and using a fish slice and moving the pan, encourage the mix into small circles.
8. Cook over a medium heat for 2 minutes each side.
9. Take out the warmed baking sheet, and turn off the oven.
10. Place each cooked blini onto the sheet to keep warm whilst you cook the remaining blinis. (Replace back in the residual heat of the oven if you need to).
11. Each blini should be served covered with red caviar, topped with a Tbsp soured cream and a sprinkle of chives.
12. Serve immediately whilst the blinis are still warm.

Olivier Salad

This is a wonderful dish for using up leftovers from the previous day. Perhaps Mrs Patmore would retain some of the chicken used to make a pie, or a roast, maybe. A ham hock also works very well with this dish.

Ingredients:

- 5 potatoes
- 3 carrots
- 4 eggs
- 1 pound boiled meat
- 1/2 lb (275g) green peas
- 2-3 dill pickles (you can use fresh cucumbers)
- Salt to taste
- 1/2 lb (275g) mayonnaise

Directions:

1. Peel and chop the potatoes and carrots, and boil until tender. In the last two minutes of cooking add the peas to cook through. Drain and set aside.
2. Bring a pan of water to the boil, and add your eggs. Cook for 7 minutes, and then plunge them into cold water to quickly cool and prevent them from over cooking. This ensures beautiful, yellow cooked yolks.
3. Chop up the meat and eggs, and mix in a bowl with the vegetables.
4. Only stir in enough mayonnaise for the dish, as any leftovers keep better without it.
5. Season to taste, and serve on a large platter, garnished with the pickles.

Russian Borscht

Ingredients:

- 3 medium-sized beetroots (uncooked)
- 1 onion
- 2 sticks of celery
- 3 pt (1.7 l) water
- 4 egg yolks
- 1 tsp lemon juice
- 1 oz (25g) butter
- Salt and pepper
- Fried croutons to serve

Directions:

1. Wash and chop the beetroots, onion, and celery.
2. Add to a large saucepan, and fry gently in the butter for around 5 minutes.
3. Add the water, bring to the boil, and then reduce to a simmer. Cook for around 1 hour.
4. Daisy would have rubbed the mixture through a sieve, but feel free to blitz smooth with a food processor.
5. Measure how much soup you have made in a jug.
6. Return to the pan, and add the lemon juice.
7. Reduce the flame to a very low heat
8. Beat the eggs lightly, and for every ½ a pint of liquid, add one yolk. Stir in each one carefully, ensuring they do not scramble, but leaving them to thicken your ruby soup
9. Serve with the fried croutons.

Palestine Soup

It is important not to confuse the ingredients of this dish with the globe artichoke. The Jerusalem artichoke is not, in fact an artichoke at all, but rather a derivative of the sunflower family! Likewise despite the name of the vegetable, neither is it from the Holy Land either. Instead its name originates from the Italian word for sunflower, *girasole*.

It is still easy to find this vegetable, but in 1920s England, it was always found in the veggie patch because the tubers were also an excellent, cheap fodder for the pigs, cattle, and chickens. It's pretty yellow flowers cheered up the garden no end, and because it has quite dense foliage, it would be used to suppress weeds too.

It is the tuber that we eat. It has a nutty, fresh crunchiness to it.

Ingredients:

- 1 ½ lb (1 kg) Jerusalem Artichokes
- 1 onion
- 1 small turnip
- ½ head of celery
- 2 small potatoes
- 1 cup (275ml) of white stock
- 1/2 cup (110ml) milk
- ¾ cup (145ml) cream
- Cayenne pepper and salt

Directions:

1. Peel and chop the vegetables finely, and place in a heavy bottomed pan.
2. Cover with the stock, and bring to the boil.
3. Reduce to a simmer, and cook for about an hour or until the vegetables have all softened.
4. Either rub through a sieve, or blitz with the food processor.
5. Return to the pan, add milk and cream, cook on a low heat until thickened slightly, but do not allow it to return to the boil.

Melba Toast

Ingredient:

- 1 thin slice of white bread per person

Directions:

1. Preheat the oven to Gas Mark 4 / 170°C / 325°F
2. Take slices of white bread, and using a serrated knife, very carefully cut through them horizontally to make two even thinner slices.
3. Place into the oven, and bake for about 4 minutes. They will turn golden brown and will curl up at the edges slightly to make lovely little boats to sail on your soup. Melba toast are also delicious served with paté.

Imitation Foie Gras

Ingredients:

- ½ lb (275g) calf's liver
- ½ lb (275g) mashed potato
- 1 small onion
- 1 oz (25g) fatty bacon
- 2 egg yolks
- ½ tsp mixed herbs
- 1 bay leaf
- ½ gill (75ml) of stock
- Salt and pepper

Directions:

1. Wash and dry your liver, and cut into small pieces
2. Chop the bacon (including fat and rind), and gently fry over a medium heat. Add the liver to the pot, and continue to fry until it lightly browned all over.
3. Add the onion, bay leaf, herbs, and stir well. Cover with stock, and bring to the boil.
4. Reduce the heat to a simmer, season to taste.
5. Leave the pot to cook until the liver is tender.
6. Mrs Patmore would pound it in a mortar, but again, a food processor works well.
7. When pulped, add the mashed potato and blitz again, or rub through a sieve.
8. Serve with Melba toast.

Baked Scallops

This dish allows for three scallops per person. Ask your fishmonger to sell you them with their shells, but ask him to remove and beard them for you. Use homemade breadcrumbs rather than the bright orange shop-bought ones.

Ingredients:

- 1 dozen scallops
- 2 oz (50g) butter
- Breadcrumbs
- Lemon juice
- Parsley

Directions:

1. Preheat your oven to 350-375°F / 180°c/ Gas 4-5
2. Grease an oven proof dish, and then coat the bottom of it with breadcrumbs to about a ¼ inch thick.
3. Now place the scallops on top, season over their surface, and add a good squeeze of lemon juice
4. Now coat with another layer of breadcrumbs, but not as thick this time.
5. Chop the butter finely, and dot it all over the top of the dish.
6. Bake for between 20 – 25 minutes.
7. Return to their shells, and garnish with fresh chopped parsley

Trout and Almonds

The gamekeeper kept the dining table at Downton Abbey well stocked from the river running through the estate. When you speak to your fishmonger about your trout, ask him to remove the fins but leave the head and tail intact.

Ingredients:

- 2 Trout
- 1 oz (25g) butter
- 2 oz (50g) ground almonds
- 1 wineglass of white wine
- Parsley
- Salt and pepper

Directions:

1. Preheat the oven to Gas 4-5 / 350-375°F / 180°C
2. Wash and dry your fish, and place it into a well-buttered, oven proof dish.
3. Season the fish well.
4. Melt your butter, and add the ground almonds to make a paste.
5. Smear the paste all over the fish.
6. Fill the dish with the wine.
7. Cover with a lid (use foil if you don't have a lid, but ensure that it is tucked under the sides well to capture the cooking powers of the steam)
8. Bake in the oven for about 30 minutes, and then serve garnished with parsley.

Sweetbreads on Ramequins

Ingredients:

- 3 Calves' sweetbreads
- 3 Bacon rashers
- 2 oz (50g) mushrooms
- Breadcrumbs
- 1 ½ Tbsp melted butter
- 1 ½ Tbsp chopped sweet herbs
- Paprika pepper

Directions:

1. Preparing sweetbreads
2. Soak in cold water for an hour.
3. Blanche in a small pan with just enough water to cover and a Tbsp lemon juice
4. Cook gently for 5 minutes, then plunge into clean, cold water.
5. This loosens all the membranes and fats, allowing you to clean them, leaving only the fleshy insides.
6. Preheat oven to 350-375°F / 180°C/ Gas 4-5
7. Cut each sweetbread into 4 pieces, and wrap a thin strip of bacon round each one.
8. Prepare a mix of breadcrumbs, seasoning, and herbs, and line each of the ramequins with a layer, then drizzle over some of the melted butter.

9. Place the sweetbread into the mix, and cover with more breadcrumbs

10. Place the ramequins onto a baking tray, and into the oven to bake for about 12 minutes or until golden brown.

Remove

(This is the formal name for the main course.)

Oxtail Casserole

I am glad to say that oxtails now come ready jointed, which means you no longer have to go at them with a cleaver! They are the beefiest beef flavour and are without compare on cold winter days.

Ingredients:

- 1 oxtail
- 1/2lb (275g) bacon
- 2 onions
- 3 carrots
- 2 turnips
- 1 bay leaf
- A small sprig of basil

Directions:

1. Toss your oxtail in flour, and fry off in a skillet. Don't be afraid to let the flour turn really golden brown because these caramelised bits really add depth to the taste of the sauce.
2. Place the singed oxtail into the base of a casserole dish. Roughly chop the vegetables, and arrange on top of the meat. Add the herbs.
3. Deglaze the pan with a tiny splash of red wine, and then add some water to rinse. Pour the liquid into the casserole pot to cover the meat and vegetables.
4. Lay the bacon over.

5. Cover the top of the casserole with foil, then place on the lid. This will prevent too much moisture from escaping.
6. Put into a slow oven. Gas mark 2 150C. 300F for four to five hours. Check regularly to ensure the liquid does not dry out.
7. Serve with boiled haricot beans.

Quail on toasts

You might want to supplement quail for partridge for this dish. This dish is best made in late summer when the leaves on the grape vines are still fresh and tender.

If you struggle to find vine leaves, a cabbage leaf will do the same job.

Ingredients:

- 1 quail per person
- 1 vine leaf per person
- 1 rasher of bacon per bird.
- 1 slice bread per person
- 1 oz (25g) of butter.

Directions:

1. Truss the quail, lay the vine leaf over the breast, place a rasher of bacon over, and secure with string.
2. Toast your bread and butter it well on one side.
3. Place the slices of toast in a roasting tray, then put one bird on top of each.
4. Cook in a hot oven 180C, 350F Gas Mark 4 for 15 minutes.
5. Put gravy onto your server.
6. Then place the quails with the toast under then, onto the gravy, then surround with watercress.

Chicken Valencia

Ingredients:

- 1 wineglass of oil
- 1 chicken, jointed and skin on.
- 6 oz (150g) rice
- 2 whole cloves of garlic
- 1 onion, thinly sliced
- 3 red chillies, thinly chopped and seeds removed
- 6 tomatoes, quartered
- 1pt (568ml) chicken stock
- Pinch of saffron

Directions:

1. Pour the oil into a flame-proof casserole with the garlic. Cook gently, being careful not to burn the garlic (which will make the dish bitter). Stir continually until the garlic is fried.
2. Now add the chicken joints to the pot. Let them fry well, but stir often so they do not burn or stick.
3. Then add the sliced onion and chillies, stirring continually.
4. Add the tomatoes, a sprinkle of parley, then add in the rice. Stir well to ensure every grain is covered with the juices.
5. Cover the whole thing with hot stock (add more, or water if needed)
6. The pan must be left open, do not cover. (Open the window. You will have quite a lot of steam.)
7. Bring to the boil, then leave the burner n, but take the pan off it, and leave it just to the side so it keeps

warm but will not burn. The rice will cook in the residual warmth.

8. Sprinkle in the saffron, and stir one last time.
9. Take to the table, and serve with chutney sandwiches made with brown bread and butter.

Fillet du Boeuf a la Carlsbad

This is rich American dish bought back from Carlsbad in California, no doubt by the delicious Martha Levinson. Never one to kowtow to convention, Martha would adore this uber sweet and sophisticated dish with a sassy kick that gets you when you least expect it.

Ingredients:

- 1 lb (454g) Sirloin of beef (Ask the butcher to prepare the undercut for you.)
- Horseradish sauce (See the recipes in the sauce section.)
- Red Currant Jelly

Directions:

1. Cut the beef into slices of about ¼ inch thick
2. Season and fry them in butter
3. Serve onto a silver dish, and pour horseradish sauce over them.
4. Decorate around the side of the platter with redcurrant jelly.
5. In a separate dish, serve a compôte of cherries as an accompaniment.

Lemon Stuffed Shoulder of Mutton

In the 1920s, mutton was far more popular than lamb. Taken from the adult sheep, it was more flavoursome and tender than lamb, as well as being a more affordable option. It had the advantage of needing to be cooked very slowly to stop it becoming tough, meaning Mrs Patmore could get this part of the dinner out of the way very early, leave it to cook, and get on with the more intricate entrées.

Strangely, in the late seventies, it seemed to drop out of favour in England, but recently it is experiencing a renaissance, I am glad to say. Replace with lamb if need be, but if you can find mutton, do try it. It is a meat in a class of its own, and of course a fraction of the price.

Ingredients:

- 1 Shoulder of mutton
- ¼ lb (125g) breadcrumbs
- 1 oz (25g) chopped suet
- 2 oz (50g) of bacon, finely chopped
- 1 egg
- 1 tsp chopped parsley
- ½ tsp chopped lemon peel.

Directions:

1. Preheat the oven to Gas Mark 4-5 / 375°F / 180°C degrees.
2. Bone the shoulder.
3. Make a stuffing with the breadcrumbs, suet, bacon, parsley, and lemon peel. Bring together with the egg.

4. Follow the line where the bone had been, covering in stuffing.
5. Roll the mutton up, and tie up very tightly with string.
6. Reduce the oven heat to 150°C 300F Gas Mark 2 and roast for 1½ hours, basting regularly.

Beef Stroganoff

Ingredients:

- 1 lb (500g) fillet steak
- 1 tsp paprika
- Zest of 1 lemon, grated
- 1 red onion, chopped
- 1 garlic clove, chopped
- Olive oil
- 2 handfuls of wild mushrooms, cleaned and torn
- Knob of butter
- Small glass of brandy
- 2 oz (50ml) sour cream
- 2–3 flat-leaf parsley sprigs, leaves picked and chopped
- Bread and gherkins, to serve

Directions:

1. Using a meat tenderiser, place the steak between two sheets of cling film, and flatten to about ½ cm, 1/8th inch thickness. Then cut the steak into finger strips of about 1cm across.
2. Make a marinade of paprika, the zest of the lemon, and salt and pepper, and smear all over the meat.
3. Fry your onion and garlic with a small amount of oil, in a heavy skillet over a medium to low heat. Be mindful of not burning the garlic as it will make the dish taste bitter. When they are softened and translucent, add the mushrooms. Turn up the heat and sauté quickly until golden brown.
4. Set the onions and mushrooms aside in a dish for a moment while you cook your meat.

5. Replenish a little more oil, and add the meat. Have the heat high so the outside of the steak browns and caramelises, but the inside remains pink. Stir the onions and mushrooms, then add the brandy. Cook for two minutes, allowing the liquid to reduce to almost nothing.
6. Remove from the heat, and stir in the cream and chopped parsley.
7. Either serve with boiled rice or with crusty bread and side order of gherkins.

Chicken Stuffed with Oysters

Ingredients:

- 1 large chicken
- 1 veal sweetbread
- 1 ½ dozen oysters
- ½ dozen mushrooms
- 2 fat bacon rashers
- 1 egg yolk
- 1 oz (25g) butter
- ½ oz (10g) flour
- 2 oz (50g) goose fat / lard
- ½ tsp parsley
- Grated ½ lemon rind
- ¼ Nutmeg, grated
- ½ pt (280g) mushroom sauce
- Salt and pepper

Preparing sweetbreads

Directions:

1. Soak in cold water for an hour.
2. Blanche in a small pan with just enough water to cover, and add Tbsp lemon juice
3. Cook gently for 5 minutes, then plunge into clean cold water.
4. This loosens all the membranes and fats, allowing you to clean them, leaving only the fleshy insides.
5. Prepare the sweetbread, and then chop it finely.
6. Roughly chop half the oysters

7. Chop the mushrooms, and mix through with the parsley, lemon rind, nutmeg and seasoning.
8. Bind the mix together with the beaten egg yolk, and then use the mix to stuff the breast of the chicken.
9. Now fill the cavity of the bird with the remaining oysters.
10. Cover the breast with the fatty bacon to keep it moist.
11. Place into roasting tin, with the 2 oz (50g) of fat.
12. Roast for 1- 1¼ hours, basting frequently.
13. About 20 minutes before the end of cooking, remove the bacon, and sprinkle the bird with flour. Pour over with melted butter to really brown the breast well.
14. Return the bird to the oven for the remaining 20 minutes.
15. Remove the trussing string, and place on a large charger.
16. Serve with a gravy boat full of mushroom sauce.

Ham Braised with Wine

This is a spectacular dish that will serve many people in one sitting with the minimum amount of fuss. It is a long cook but easy, and the meat melts in your party mouth like nothing you have ever tasted! This was a perfect dish for an elaborate event like New Year's Eve when Mrs Patmore would want to enjoy her own celebrations, but nevertheless put on a breathtakingly impressive spread.

A York Ham was envied across the British Empire. The meat, left on the bone, had been dry cured for 10 weeks and then breaded. It was drier and saltier than any made anywhere else in the kingdom. Now of course, there is no need to preserve meats like this, and sadly, this is only really seen for sale as a speciality item. When I make this dish, I use a large, regular ham, or gammon, as we call it, which has the same salty edge.

Ingredients:

- 1 York Ham soaked (Americans can substitute with a Smithfield, or other type of country ham)
- ½ pt (280ml) Espagnole Sauce
- 1 pt (568ml) chicken stock
- ½ pt (280ml) sherry or Masala wine
- ½ pt (280ml) Champagne

Directions:

1. Soak the ham for 24-48 hours in cold water. Change the water at least twice.
2. Put the ham into a large pot with just enough stock to cover.

3. Bring the water to the boil. Some white froth will start to come to the surface.
4. Skim it off, and reduce the pan to a simmer.
5. Cook for 3-4 hours, skimming the surface regularly.
6. Remove the ham from its juices, and take off its skin.
7. Place into a clean pan, with the juices and the wines.
8. Cook very gently for 40 minutes.
9. Remove from the pan, and set aside covered with foil to keep warm.
10. Now skim the stock very thoroughly, and reduce to half the quantity.
11. Add the espagnole sauce gently, stir, and bring it back to the boil.
12. Place the ham on a large serving charger surrounded with a little of the sauce and rest in a gravy boat at the side.

Vegetables Dishes

Asparagus Moulds

Ingredients:

- Small bundle of fresh asparagus
- 2 oz (50g) butter
- 1 pt (568ml) Bechamel sauce
- 2 egg yolks
- 1 tbs Vegetable stock

Directions:

1. First begin by making your béchamel sauce.
2. Chop the asparagus into small pieces, and drop them into salted boiling water.
3. Boil for 5 minutes.
4. Melt the butter and season with salt and paper. Stir the butter into the béchamel, and simmer it gently for 5 minutes allowing it to thicken.
5. Remove from the heat, and leave to cool very slightly.
6. Add a tablespoon of stock, and beat in the egg yolks one at a time, being careful the mix is cool enough not to cause your eggs to scramble.
7. Stir in the asparagus.
8. Put into butter moulds or ramekins, then pour in the mix.
9. Place into a roasting tin, and then fill the tin with hot water to about halfway up the mould. Stand in the tin until the water goes cold.
10. Ensure the sauce has set solid before turning out onto places.

Polish red cabbage

Ingredients:

- 1 red cabbage
- 1 sour apple
- 1 onion
- ½ oz (10g) butter
- 1 tbs brown sugar
- 1 tsp ground cinnamon
- 1 tsp powdered cloves

Directions:

1. Slice the cabbage into small pieces
2. Peel and slice the apple and onion in small chunks too.
3. Place into a saucepan with just enough water to prevent it burning, as well as the butter.
4. Simmer gently, and when cooked, season with the sugar, spices, and vinegar (which will give it that ruby red finish).

Sauces

Redcurrant Jelly

This recipe is taken from "***Christmas at Downton***," giving you one of several other ways to use your jar in other dishes!

Makes 1 litre or 2 lb jelly

The simplest of recipes made from the fruit from the estate. Many fruity delights would have been canned to preserve the crops, meaning they were ready to improve dishes at a moment's notice. This is used in the Fillet du Boeuf a la Carlsbad, but it's just as delicious served with roast lamb or duck or melted into gravies to make rich sauces.

The reason this is so easy is that there is no messing about with stalks. Place everything into the pan to stew, and then simply strain through a muslin bag to create a clear ruby jelly.

Ingredients:

- 2 lb (900g) Redcurrants
- 2 lb (900g) Sugar

Directions:

1. Place the berries into a heavy-bottomed pan.
2. Squash them as well as you can to release the juices.
3. Slowly bring to the boil, then add the sugar.
4. Boil fast for 8 minutes.
5. Meanwhile, wash your jars and lids. Boil the lids for 5 minutes, and place the jars into a hot oven to dry and sterilise. (Mind how you remove them!)

6. Make a muslin bag by lining a sieve with fabric and placing over a jug.
7. Pour the redcurrant concoction through, and leave it to drip. The more you force it through, the cloudier the jelly, but of course it makes more too, so decide which suits you best.
8. Pour into pots, and cover with wax discs when cooled. Put the lids on, and label with satisfaction. Store in a cool, dry place until needed.

Espagnole Sauce

This looks like a complicated cook, but on closer examination you will see it is a "Sumthin' outta Nuthin'" dish. It uses leftovers to make a great pantry cupboard staple that takes fairly simple dishes into something truly extraordinary.

Ingredients:

- 4 oz (125g) Veal
- 2 oz (50g) Ham
- 1 onion
- 1 carrot
- ¼ head of celery
- 2 oz (50g) butter
- 2 oz (50g) flour
- 3 pt (1.7l) stock
- Remains of leftover chicken
- 1 gill (142ml) tomato purée
- A large bunch of herbs
- ½ dozen peppercorns, Crushed
- 1 blade of mace, crushed
- 2 oz (50g) mushrooms, chopped
- ½ gill (75ml) claret
- ½ wineglass sherry
- Salt and pepper

Directions:

1. Peel and cut up all of the vegetables.
2. Chop the ham and veal.

3. Melt a little butter in a skillet, and add all the vegetables (excluding mushrooms) gently until they are soft and very slightly browned.
4. Add all of the meats, the herbs, the peppercorns, and spices.
5. Stir over a low flame until browned and any fats have been released.
6. Drain off the fats, stir trough the tomato purée, the mushrooms and wine, then add the stock.
7. Now, take another pan and melt together the butter and the flour, mixing to a roux.
8. Gradually add the stock to the roux, mixing in at each step.
9. As the sauce comes together, bring it to the boil, and simmer for an hour.
10. Skim the surface regularly, then pass through a sieve lined with muslin.
11. Decant into sterile bottles. This will keep several weeks in the refrigerator.

Mushroom Sauce

Ingredients:

- 1 1b button mushrooms
- ½ pt (280ml) beef stock
- 1 oz (25g) butter
- 1 oz (25g) flour
- 1 tsp celery salt
- 1 tsp lemon juice
- Salt and pepper

Directions:

1. Peel and chop the mushrooms, and cook in the stock with celery salt and seasoning until tender.
2. In another pan, melt the butter, and add to make a roux.
3. Remove from the heat
4. Gradually add the mushroom mix to the roux, stirring well to absorb all of the liquor before adding the next bit.
5. Return to the heat, add the lemon juice, and bring to the boil. Simmer for 5 minutes before serving.

Horseradish Sauce

Ingredients:

- One young fresh horseradish root
- 2 tsp Castor sugar
- 1 tbs Vinegar
- Salt
- 1 pt (568ml) Cream

Directions:

1. Grate the root very finely.
2. Stir in the sugar and vinegar
3. Add salt to taste
4. Slacken with the cream, adding gradually to ensure just the right texture.
5. Horseradish should be served cold with cold meats and warmed with hot.
6. To warm the sauce, put in a jug, and place the jug in warmed water.
7. (If you want to use up a glut of horseradish and preserve it to keep, replace the cream with vegetable oil and grated orange peel and keep in a sterilised jar).

Cherry Compôte

Ingredients:

- 1 lb (454g) Cherries (pitted)
- ½ cup (200g) Sugar
- 1 quart (1.1 l) cold water
- 1 tbs Arrowroot
- Juice of ½ lemon
- 3 fl oz (100ml) Cherry brandy

Directions:

1. Place the stoned cherries into a heavy saucepan, and cover with water, then bring them to a rolling boil.
2. Add the sugar, and continue to boil until the fruit has softened.
3. Pass the mixture through a sieve, and retain the pulp.
4. Mix the arrowroot to a paste with a little cold water.
5. Put the fruit pulp back onto the heat, and quickly add in the arrowroot, stirring all of the time. The mixture will go milky, and as it cooks through, will become jewel clear.
6. Add in the lemon juice, and taste. If needed, add a little more sugar to sweeten.
7. Take off the heat, and stir in the brandy.

Bechamel Sauce

Ingredients:

- ¾ pint (180ml) of vegetable stock (or chicken in the recipe better warrants it)
- ½ pt (280ml) milk
- 2 oz (50g) butter
- 1 oz (25g) flour
- 6 peppercorns
- 1 carrot
- 1 onion

Directions:

1. Parsley and a bay leaf, salt and pepper.
2. Boil the stock up with the carrot, the onion (cut into two halves to release the flavour), and the peppercorns. Reduce the stock to about half, then strain.
3. Melt the butter in a pan, and work the flour in to a smooth paste.
4. Heat the milk, and gradually add the stock and the milk in small amounts, each time absorbing all of the liquid into the paste.
5. Season with salt and paper.

Desserts

Summer Pudding

This dish has been a favourite in English homes for hundreds of years. It's interesting because it is sumptuous but truly is a "free food" pudding. Nowadays, our bread if full of flour improvers and additives which mean it will last longer, but Mrs Patmore would always be on the lookout for ways to get better value for money from her loaves. When the hedgerows were heaving with fruit, this was the perfect treat to use up yesterday's bread.

Ingredients:

- ½ lb (275g) blackcurrants, raspberries redcurrants or strawberries
- Slices of bread and butter
- Sugar
- ½ pt (280ml) cream

Directions:

1. You can use any fruit you like really, and sometimes I add some small chunks of apple into mine. Stew the fruit gently, taking into consideration that apples and pears will take longer than berries. Add sugar to taste as they are beginning to soften, but do not make the mix too sweet.
2. Mrs Patmore greased her bowl well to get the pudding to slip out easily, but now lining the bowl with cling film will give you a similar but healthier effect! I find it easiest to use two long pieces

crisscrossed over the bowl, to overlap. Leave yourself about 15 cm on each end to help you compress the pudding at the end.

3. Take thin slices of bread and butter, and cut off the crusts so you have rectangular shapes, but angle then slightly so they seem to lean. This will help you get a better fit in the bowl. Aim for four slices, cut into two rectangles each, and 2 slices cut into 4 triangles each.

4. Find a heavy pudding basin. Taking the rectangular bread pieces, one at a time, dip them gently in the fruit juices, and then use them to line the inside with the bread and butter (the butter facing into the pudding). Take time over it filling any cracks and fitting the bread closely and tightly together.

5. Using a slotted spoon, fill the bread basin halfway up with fruit, then make a lid with some of the triangles of bread, so it acts a bit like scaffolding, ready for you to add more fruit on top.

6. Fill to the top with the rest of the fruit, then cover with a final whole piece of bread and butter, firmly sealing all the fruit and juices in.

7. The remaining juices should be kept for serving later.

8. Use kitchen scissors to trim away excess bits of bread and neaten the edges.

9. Place a plate over the top so it weights the bread and squashes and forms the putting.

10. Put it into the fridge to chill overnight.

11. When you come to serve, turn out onto a place and cover with lashings of cream (whether it is whipped or not is up to you) and drizzle the juice on the serving plate around it. A true, summer ruby treasure.

Crème on Surprise

This is an unusual dish that seems to have been lost in the annals of time. It is scrumptious and looks amazing on the table, and never fails to impress. Part of the reason we may not see it very often now is that we have to do our own washing up…and preparing this dish makes loads, I will warn you! Make sure you have your very own Daisy to do the clearing up!

Ingredients:

- 2 eggs
- 4 oz (125g) sugar
- 2 oz (50g) self-rising flour
- 1 oz (25g) corn flour
- 1 gill (142ml) cream
- ½ oz (10g) butter
- 6 oz (170g) apricot jam
- 2 oz (50g) walnuts
- 3 oz (75g) glacé cherries
- 1 wineglass of sherry
- Vanilla extract
- Lemon juice1
- 1/3 cup (100ml) of water.

Directions:

1. Preheat the oven too Gas Mark 5/ 375 F/ 180C
2. Grease an ovenproof dish, and sprinkle with flour.
3. Take three mixing bowls.
4. Separate your eggs, yolks into one bowl and whites into another.

5. In the first bowl, cream together the yolks of the eggs with 2 oz (50g) of the sugar, then stir in a few drops of vanilla extract.
6. In the second bowl, sieve together the flour and the corn flour.
7. Take bowl number three, and whisk your egg whites to stiff peaks. When you confidently hold the bowl upside down over your head and know they will stay firmly there, you know you have reached the right consistency!
8. Now gradually and alternately add the flour mix and the egg whites into your yolk mix. Use a metal spoon to gently fold it in so you don't knock out any of the air.
9. Spoon the mix into your ovenproof dish, and bake for 30 minutes.
10. When it is cooked, remove from the oven, and place onto a cooling rack for 15 minutes.
11. Now cut off the top of the cake, and scoop out the middle.
12. Fill the centre of the mix of whipped cream, a tsp of sugar, the walnuts, and the cherries. Replace the lid. Place into a glass dish, or serve on a cake stand.
13. Put the jam into a pan with the water, and boil up to make a glaze.
14. Leave the glaze to cool, then add the sherry and lemon juice.
15. When the glaze is completely cold, paint or brush over the pudding, and sprinkle with pistachio nuts and some of the cherries.

Queen Mab Pudding

Just as jellies were popular on the most elegant of tables, so were other desserts moulded into elaborate shapes. This one was particularly popular for parties.

Those of you who remember your Shakespeare will be able to conjure to mind the faery queen of Mercutio's speech in Romeo and Juliet. It was said that she was the midwife of dreams, and this dish is every bit good enough to evoke that kind of reverie. They say this is the desert of witchery! It was a firm English favourite at the turn of the twentieth century.

The question is, I wonder, would her ladyship court the help of Mrs Patmore in weaving such spells at the table, or would she simply ask that it be served! Either way, this could be the perfect way to seal any deals required from the table, romantic, political, or otherwise.

Ingredients:

- 6 Egg Yolks, lightly beaten
- 1 pt (454ml) Milk
- 4 oz (125g) sugar
- 1 oz (25g) gelatine
- 1 gill (142ml) water
- 2 oz (50g) glacé cherries
- 2 oz (50g) crystalised fruits (Crystalised ginger or angelica for instance)
- 1 lemon
- Vanilla extract

Directions:

1. Grate the rind of the lemon, and place into a pan with the milk. Heat gently, and bring it to the boil.
2. Cool it for 5 minutes, then strain the milk through a sieve onto the egg yolks
3. Transfer back into the pan, and heat over a very low flame, stirring constantly to thicken to a custard. Do not let it boil.
4. Dissolve the gelatine into water, then add to the custard.
5. When the custard has cooled, add in the crystalised fruit and chopped cherries.
6. Place into the refrigerator for an hour to completely cool, then stir in the whipped cream.
7. Run your mould under the cold tap so it is completely wet, then transfer the mixture into it. This dampness will ensure the pudding comes out easily.
8. Leave in the refrigerator overnight to set.

Strawberry Soufflé

The mark of a great cook has always been, and always will be, can she get her soufflé to rise! This was a great dish for Alfred to learn to perfect ready to excel when he left to work at the Ritz.

This is a summer-only recipe, when English strawberries are at their very finest. Either cook in one large soufflé dish or in a 4 or 5 ovenproof ramekins.

Ingredients:

- 3/4 lb (325g) strawberries
- 2 oz (50g) sugar
- 1 oz (25g) flour
- 2 eggs
- 1 oz (25g) butter
- 1 gill (142ml) of milk
- Red food colouring

Directions:

1. Preheat oven Gas 6-7 / 400°F- 425°F/ 200°C
2. Squeeze half of the strawberries through a sieve to make a pulp, then add 1 oz (25g) sugar to sweeten the fruit.
3. Melt the butter in a pan, gradually add the flour, and bring it together to make a roux.
4. Little by little, add the milk, always taking time to stir it enough so the milk disappears into the roux before adding the next bit of liquid.

5. Bring the sauce together, and let it boil gently and thicken, then add the other 1 oz (25g) of sugar and the strawberry pulp.
6. Separate your eggs. Beat the yolks together well, and add a couple of drops of food colouring.
7. Whisk the egg whites to stiff peaks (use the same trick to test as in the crème di surprise recipe).
8. Fold the stiff whites into the yolks gradually with a metal spoon, and also add the rest of the thinly sliced strawberries
9. Butter a soufflé dish well, then add the mix
10. Place into a preheated oven for 25 - 30 minutes.
11. Do not be tempted to open the oven door before 25 minutes or your soufflé will flop.
12. Serve to the table in its dish.

Cocktails

Hedgerow Hangover!

This recipe perfectly sums up the feeling of the era. It captures the seasonality of the glut in the hedgerows (England is covered in the milking cream flowers of the Elder on Midsummer's day) with the love of the Russian immigration influences.

Serve in a classic champagne saucer (the triangular-shaped ones, rather than flutes).

Ingredients:

- 1 fl oz (25ml) vodka
- ½ fl oz (15ml) elderflower cordial
- Champagne

Directions:

1. Add the vodka and the elderflower cordial to a cocktail shaker with lots of ice.
2. Shake well.
3. Take your glass, and dip the rim in egg white then into sugar to give a frosting.
4. Add the elderflower mix, and top up with champers!
5. Chin chin!

Gin Rickey

Ingredients:

- Ice cubes
- Limes
- Gin
- Soda

Directions:

1. Add 3 or 4 four ice cubes to a tall glass
2. Squeeze half the juice of the lime into the glass, rub the rim of the glass with juice, and then drop the remaining wedges into glass
3. Add 2 oz (50g) Gin.
4. Top with soda to taste.

Mint Julep

This is a great recipe for using up leftover champagne or sparkling wine because the sugar reactivates the fizz.

Ingredients:

- 5–10 sprigs of mint, plus 1 to garnish
- ½ fl oz (15ml) sugar syrup
- 1 dash lime juice
- Champagne, to top up

Direction:

1. Place the mint, lime juice and sugar syrup into a long tumbler, add crushed ice, and top up with champagne. Garnish with a floating mint leaf.

Conclusion

Thanks so much for taking this nostalgic journey with me, and I hope to see in the reviews of the successes of the dishes you have made. It would be lovely to think we could resurrect some of the great wonders of the culinary world like Queen Mab's pudding and Espagnole Sauce.

I dearly hope you have enjoyed your foray into how "the other half lived." I wonder if we will ever get back to those ways of dining again. Clearly, when you look at the amount of butter and cream, I think most of us would balk at such excess in one sitting, but the elegant menus are so beautiful, aren't they?

What's more I think there is a lot to be learned from how long the aristocracy took eating their food. They had time to listen to each other, to know what was happening in each other's lives. Well, clearly, those would be the bits they wanted each other to know any way!

Whist the food bill of a house such as Downton was large, by today's standards it could be considered modest. Food was seen as an asset, and England lived by the mantra "Waste not, want not." The food on the table went a very long way.

This book is a snapshot into how life was to change, really. It was the end of a beautiful era of which my nation is incredibly proud, but the class system very rightly was coming to an end. For all the good that brought in terms of better healthcare, better jobs, and improved education, we mourn the passing of great traditions of grandeur such as these.

With tradition, of course, came onerous standards of etiquette. If you would be interested in knowing more about seating dictates, cutlery layout, and indeed the almost scientific rules of table decoration of the era, you might want to read "***Christmas at Downton***" where I have covered this at length.

If, like me, you have a sweet tooth and enjoy a little something of what you fancy, why don't you join me for **"*Tea at Downton*"** too?

Elizabeth Fellow

Check out Elizabeth's other books!!!

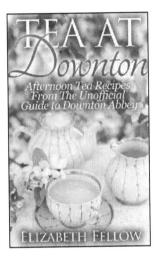

http://www.amazon.com/dp/B00I5ASVX0

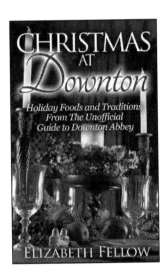

http://www.amazon.com/dp/B00P1RP9VM

Made in the USA
Lexington, KY
19 March 2015